Floating Girl (Angel of War)

Copyright © 2006 by Robert Randolph. All rights reserved.

Author Photo: Amy Randolph

Cover Art: *Le Jeune Martyr* by Paul Delaroche,
used courtesy of the Louvre, Paris

Book Design: Joel A. Bass

ISBN: 1-932418-17-2

Elixir Press
PO Box 27029
Denver, Colorado 80227

www.ElixirPress.com

Elixir Press is a nonprofit literary organization.

Floating Girl
(Angel of War)

ROBERT RANDOLPH

ELIXIR PRESS

"I read Floating Girl (Angel of War) after exiting the hush of Anne Frank's Secret Annex, and no poetry could have been more pertinent to my private insistence on honoring not only Anne, the dreaming child whose hope and candor the world has come to embrace, but Anne the sacrificed, the betrayed girl who died, emaciated and bereft in Bergen-Belsen. The specter of war's innumerable Annes, of the red-covered infant ("this child needed our lips on her lips") haunts and suffuses this fearless, necessary, and ennobling book. Bell-clear and heartbreaking, superbly imagistic (Paul Celan's "Death Fugue" and Picasso's "Guernica" come to mind), Bob Randolph's piercing and prayerful lament mines a realm of utter grief and moral obscenity with assiduous craft and compassionate fire. It is a work of extraordinary love, dignity, and spiritual acuity, and I admire it enormously."

Cyrus Cassels

Acknowledgments

Acknowledgement is given to the following publications in which some of these poems have appeared previously.

Blueline for Part One of "Idols" (as "Discovery on a Hillside")

The Carleton Miscellany for "The Son She Left" (as "The Purer Part").

Margie: The American Journal of Poetry for "Psalm 10," "Psalm 12," and "To the Generals."

Imported Breads (Mammoth Press) for "A Modest Proposal" (as "Dead Children"), and parts of "The Finland Suite."

Poetry East for "Poem for Garcia Lorca" (part of "Trying to Find Joy, Circa 1969"), and Part 1 of "How I Feel" (as "White Cups)

Zuzu's Petals for "Wool Coat" (part of "Trying to Find Joy")

"Floating Girl (Angel of War)" was 2003 winner of the War Poetry Prize given by WinningWriters.com and appears on that web site as 2003 winner.

Table of Contents

I. Floating Girl

Floating Girl (Angel of War)	3
Psalm 10	5
Psalm 12	6
To the Generals	8
Archive of Death	9
Of Jesus	10
Knife Blades	13
Waiting for a Place to Shine	14
Measuring the Silence	15
Psalm 24	16
After Rain	18
Moths	19
A Modest Proposal	20

II. Distant Roads

    The Finland Suite   25

    Three Photos   30

III. The Ticking of Snow

    To the Rich   35

    The Ticking of Snow   36

    Icons   38

    Photo of a Burial Bag   40

IV. Trying to Take Joy

    Trying to Find Joy, Circa 1969   45

    The Son She Left, 1977   47

    How I Feel   48

I. Floating Girl

Floating Girl (Angel of War)

> *"...doubling up in pain like a river*
> *with these white flowers...."*
> —Jose Louis Hidalgo

Floating face down,
she is part of the river's script of bodies,
its holy marginalia.

Her head floats inside her own hair.
Her body drifts in moonlight, in privacy beyond rain: the hour has lost its shoreline.
You want to kiss her, but your lips are glass; your handkerchief has turned to white glass.

A prayer wheel is turning. You want to give her palomino ponies with golden hooves.
She cannot wait, floating downstream.
Already her sky fills part of the western horizon.

Her upper back breaks the surface.
You can hear the bell of silence near her skin.

*

She is not alone.
Some die in a silence that rises up from their feet,
like a bitter, dumb angel. Finally, there is nothing left of them to hear.

No one knows the location of every child's body, inventing their small books to give to God.
The bones of these children are made of silence.
They saw darkness fly into the mirror.

The shadows, already folded, fold again.
Children's bodies lie in the rain, badly dressed night-birds, and only their names get up.
The bones of murdered babies drift so far, no gloves can lift them.
Nothing puts out their light. They burn like plants, in the distance, like harps.

*

The light is dim against your windows. There is nothing to say.
The towel lies where you left it on the stand, and you look at its texture; it seems a small
    white world.
You cover your eyes with your hands. This is enormous dignity.
You pray for children awake in shadows.

Of course you pray, because a child's love is the clearest river that flows through the human body;
you can see all its stones. The floating girl's face drifts toward the sea.
She wraps silence around herself like a scarf.

Her body rolls over and lifts its dead hand toward the moon.
A small piece of wind blows around you and closes behind you. That was her life.
Now you stand inside the oval of her death.
Your heart enters a drifting room of tulips.

Psalm 10

Of Jesus carrying a child.

You look out your window.
      The wind carries a knife in its back pocket.
Jesus enters an olive grove carrying a corpse, looking at you.

The corpse is a bombed child, yours.
      Jesus has wide eyes and shoulders, thin enough to be painted on a plate.
The child is blue, like the sea, like the sleeve of your shirt.

Jesus walked in a raw, hollow snow, only a wave, a ghost,
      wind across a white pond, toward you. He walked like a winter landscape.
You are going to church in the snow sky. The child's chest cavity lies open,

a pool of black blood. She weighs a thousand pounds;
      only Jesus can hold her now.
"Do not fear," he says, "she is asleep."

You understand she is the one who is many.
      You alone can pull her back from the many, to the one.
You must make her older, because she rushed too soon to her last category.

This is the gift of Jesus, to hold her for you.
      The music of his voice is like an underwater shadow.
To get to him, you must dive deep,

past the ancient tessellated floor where candles burn in the ornate chancel
      for the living and the dead, down to a nameless corpse.
This is migration to the land of your blood.

Psalm 12

She feared murderers hidden in her own hair.

All her doorways opened at last into her own spilled blood.
    Jesus wants you to step toward the child from the nearest horizon.
An era arrives out of heaven,

full of exile. Angels have wrapped their astonishment around this child like a robe.
    Her clothing used to be made of her parents' words.
Now her parents block their own mouths with their hands;

you've seen that in many photos. Wounds have settled too deep in everyone's mouth.
    This child needed our lips on her lips.
But the moon burned goodnight without a story or a kiss.

Her story floats toward you.
    You open the envelope of snow. It is still falling, on a stone house
near a gray river. A small wind blows.

This was her house.
    Finally she had no dresser, no clothes hangers, no toilet,
only part of a wall. A bomb fell and spoke only one word.

She believed snow would fall through every decision,
    through the expressions on anyone's face. But snow could not fall through glass,
so she tried to stand still, inside a glass tube. This is the snow falling out of her blood,
    saying her story.

All the animals left her heart.

Her leopards went underwater, to wait.
    The girl felt heaviness inside her, like wet fur.
Her big birds fell, each one like a black city, with its streets, from the sky.

It was the girl's spirit.
    It was knowing she would spend the rest of her days with sorrow in her soul.
The stones held their small cups, asking for alms.

But now there is a new coating on every stone, the fact of her death.
And so many have died a black cloth covers everything.
She wished her heart could have escaped through a hole in the sky.
    She died with that wish. Jesus hands you this child of falling snow.

To the Generals

>*"And downshore from the cloud,*
>*I stand, waiting,*
>*for dark."*
>   —James Wright

Your maps and medals, the seven buttons of your shirt,
your stone house by the river,
    a bird blown apart by a shotgun.

Pieces of daylight fit together above the icy grass.
The world hisses its way around. The ash tree
finds inner peace. The sky puts clouds between its teeth.

*

Suppose bodies of these children
    float like boats, underground. That is the river you sink your well into.

Archive of Death

> *"There's only this single body, this tiny garment*
> *gathering the past against itself...."*
> —Charles Wright

The horrible loneliness of a gold necklace on the throat of a refugee mother
whose son is dying. No one can edge our world past her silence.
It travels down, along the mirrors of rivers.
She carries her baby, and they make one flame.
She walks through rain, through particles of God, through angels.
The baby could be a piece of silver,
an icon, but it is her baby, shining in her arms like a star, a lily.
She trembles at the coastline of her own heartbeat.

This poem concerns candles in the falling snow, adults weeping in a transparent city.
The baby's death will not be absorbed by the archives of rain.

Of Jesus

For resonator guitar and snare drum.

You stand by a window, overlooking a valley in shadow,
    thinking of death as a second body.

For them, death comes as an iron-red angel.
    You don't want to name death an angel. It is more like a space, you say,
and the children drift into it.
No, they are murdered.
The angel comes out of a mirror where a man shaves his face.

You can see him from the bottom of the sea.
    Waves and wild birds spill themselves away from his horrible, bloody hands.

    There is every reason to believe he wants the sea to be blood.
    The angel rises like a wave, like a chain pulled through their eyes.
Maybe you touch the window because of this image.

Carve for these corpses ebony figurines.

    To protect the living,
        forge iron gates of Mozart arpeggios; take the orphans to tea
with old women who have walked barefoot their whole lives through African dust,
                who laugh from their chests.

    Be willing to share your veins,
offer your blood.

    They are cut from soft air. Pray for them.
Your hair darkens as you pray.
    Silence moves your forearm hair. There is no way to pity yourself.

Everything remains distant, beyond all precise darkness,
    because they walk alone, like birds flying across a winter sky.

You want Jesus to take your hands,
    to turn his face away, so you can ask, "Does rain achieve immortality,
    falling on dead children?"

"Are there divine demands behind each unique moment?"
    But you wait like a stone in failure.

*

    Prayer is a form of dignity, as you understand it, far beyond you.
Prayer is damask, thin candle flame.
But yours is the silence of one, not between two. Yours is the quiet of a cave.

You remember a hotel room in an Arab country.
There was a white pitcher of clean water, a simple gift like the moon.

    You want to feel the care of Jesus's waiting,
the king who will wait for you to perform ablutions. Several times you lift water
        against your closed eyes, and draw your fingertips
to the corners of your mouth.

    Jesus waits for you, but you have nothing to say.

    The wood table by the window has more rights than the children.
Photos of them have more rights than do their bodies.
        The truth of their pain lays aside the moonlight. Your only prayer
would be built of one color, like a red horse
        swimming in blood.

    There can be no safety,
        no way to stay in your body,
because you are drowned in the clots of their deaths, the blood sea.

*And as you wait,
Jesus prays for you.*

Knife Blades

There are no names as thin as their bodies. Flies land in their eyes.
    The last thing moving will be God's hand pinning medals on their torn clothing, on the small blankets
        wrapped around their last breath.

Waiting for a Place to Shine

       Bones of the skull showing,
the heart working behind the ribs,
    thousands of years of hope behind each heartbeat. This is the true intimacy
        of human life,
the blood always bending back to the heart's door.

Measuring the Silence

       As you put a water glass in the dish washer
look at the starving child who looks at you. This one is dying of thirst.
The *hereness* you feel moves out over the countryside like rain, but the last drops fall
    thousands of miles short of the child, who has shut her eyes.
         She will not fall asleep again.

Psalm 24

Of parents.

1-The Ones Who Cannot Forget You

We make children's bodies luminous. Every afternoon,
as we lay them down to sleep, they love the closeness of the body,
      and pay attention.

Do you remember that easy crossing to your own father and mother,
    the safe space around your bed, because of them?

You, yourself, before you slept, as a child, became suddenly loving too.
Who were these, who stayed close to the ground
      and all your life could not forget you? Around you, you felt your own sky.
      They made you safe,
so the doors stayed safely shut behind the heavy locks of sleep.

Your mother's kisses and whispers silenced your mouth,
        but now you must help grandmothers arrive,
stepping out of the yellow
photographs some children carry.

2-The Other Father

   Her whole life
surfaces into this moment. She does not understand.
      Her daddy has come apart.
      She could walk through him as through a dead city.
There is not one drawer left in him, where she could store one whisper.

Snow falls on his forehead,
as if a small king of snow commanded it. Every path coming out of his body leads nowhere.

*

        He picked her up gracefully, and carried her to bed
and she wanted to lose herself into him, holding his hand
until she slept, but he looked behind her to recent news of his brother's death in combat.
        He stroked her hair, and she felt the confusion around his wrists,
and she could not follow.

Now the walls watch her.

*

You know the man contains you; your life is his heartwood.
But in your living room the whole river of death can be polished,
        every moonlit pattern in its surface rubbed silver, but that water falls
    though the other father's fingers.

After Rain

> *"Earth revealed like this demands a dignity
> that was never in us."*
> —James Galvan

Perhaps the body prays
continually, a reed moved by water, disappearing in dark mud
where the roots sit like an old man
    alone in his kitchen after midnight.

I sit at my kitchen table. The lawn seems tender after rain.
The sky gone clear, the moon blooms.

A small herd of deer grazes by the split rail fence. I drink tea,
lifting the yellow cup with its hand-painted red dragon
to my lips.

I'm listening to Miles Davis play "Sketches of Spain,"
to me, music of prayer light,
    like waking and finding a star has fallen into my body.

But the landscape of African women
holding starving babies on their hips causes the stars to fly further off
    like a flock of white egrets!

Moths

> *"It was reported their singing resembled*
> *the flight of moths in moonlight."*
> —Denise Levertov

    Against your window, a silent affair of snow.

You know when these children die, the world is not where you left it.
Your furniture drifts toward serenity, solitude,
    fear.
    If you lit a candle its light would fold back into its light.

The child in your breathing writes you a letter.
The ink becomes a shoreline, behind it a country village with friendly dogs.
In a small house a dark woman sits, talking about horses.
    Find the child who needs you; follow the dark woman's voice.

    Start there in the winter light on your oak desk by the window,
    where children cry dimly inside the wood.

A Modest Proposal

Let's gather the war-dead children
and lay them in a river, "The River Flowing With Dead Children."
Let's charge people to stand on a footbridge
to watch the bodies twist around each other, dragging slowly downstream.
Let's make a city where the bodies empty into the sea.
The saddest place on earth, alive with gambling casinos and churches,
"The City of Goodbyes." Mystics, psychics, faith healers,
and the world's best university, on streets overlooking the roll
of faded girls and boys into deeper water.

No matter what time of day, what the news,
dead children flow into the sea. People talk on the banks about their lives,
new cars, loves, conversations deepened by parts of bodies
visibly breaking the surface. The business hours run eight to five,
motels are usually booked weeks in advance.

This river is dark, even in moonlight. Near it, lovers sit under elms,
aware of their hearts beating. The chief of police himself patrols between dusk
and dawn. There is no end of dead children.
The river sings with its bodies.

II. Distant Roads

The Finland Suite

I-Train North

1

        I took the train north
to the arctic circle,
through the white birch night.

    In one station, a chained dog barked at the train in the snow;
the face barked
      in all directions.

   A few people
boarded there. One old woman carried
            wrapped gifts.

2

      Ten people got off with me
and we walked across the tracks to town.
        I took a room and watched the traffic.
The restaurant served reindeer and bear meat.
    I ate meat pie, and drank cloudberry liquor.

   I went for a walk toward the river.

   Every building I passed
felt lonely and distant. The river was frozen, covered with snow.

   I broke into tens, then
      hundreds,
        then thousands.

Pieces of me set out in small boats, sailing through the snow
wanting to help the children.

II-Chess

1

Afternoon, I'm playing chess
with Heikki.

Varpu gave him the beautiful
Russian set
we always use, stone pieces and board.

He unpacks them and sets his side up slowly.
I face my knights and bishop's miters
carefully toward him.

2

He wears a blue sweater with a dark red rectangle
on the chest. This is a long, close game.
I look out the window
as he reconsiders. I watch
two very old women, dressed in black,
arm in arm cross the bridge into the park.

I think about castleing, if he moves his black bishop.

The women
walk past an ice covered birch tree.

  To the women
maybe nothing is happening, they are just walking.
   But to me,
they burn with beauty. They take small steps,
knees bent slightly, because of the ice.

  How much light over the years
  have they
    each brushed into the hair of children?

III-Almond Tree

  I think of an almond tree
in the front yard of a house I lived in once, in Macedonia.
I wish people
  had a key to open the past
back up, but I know under certain stars the past can catch up to the present
and they travel side by side,

  because sometimes I feel like I'm living right next to
those papery white blossoms
  here in Finland.

  I walk along the path of that feeling,
  keeping to myself,
    walking past dark stones
   washed by sea water.

  At home, I become sad for the flame of my oil lamp,
for the children,
  and for this world and myself. I sit in a corner,
my back against two walls, thinking of the faces
   of children of war in photos.
  Now the photos are all that's left.

IV-Soul of a Country

      Sleet against the windows,
  I read by a lamp, listening to Finlandia,
trying to learn about Finland's soul.
      Sibelius, they say, saw a flock of wild swans
    in his old age
and called it one of his life's great moments.

       Two nights ago, my friend Elise threw a snowball
      against my second storey window.
  I looked out and there she was in her red coat
  ready to throw another. I went down
and we went out for a few beers.

      We ran into Eero and he introduced me to his friend
who was dying, everyone thought,
    drinking himself to death. He shook my hand.
  We all talked about politics and poetry;

then he wept, quietly,
    one hand covering closed eyes, for all of us.

V-Library

    Standing by the library
       balcony railing

by the Gulf of Bothnia,
looking across
    the water
at white houses
on an island:

     the thick gloves
of winter silence touch me.

I walk back through town, past old wood buildings
     along the waterfront.

VI-Birds

1

    Three birds walk on the coffeehouse lawn.
I like their brown against the pale grass.
They seem like deserted beaches,
     empty, the sea rolling in against their sincerity.

    They also seem like distant roads,
their heads down as if knowing one thing,
     the way, like pavement.

2

    There is a pair of birds flying low over the water, away.
They seem like ink on rice paper.

    The bodies of those children are such fragile jars.

Three Photos

1

A man wearing thin white cloth carries his son
to the refugee clinic, the boy draped across his arms.
The man's face shows the broken distance
between stone and light inside the boy's body.

The son's human rights define the father's face,
a demand to be helped. This man is you, carrying
the waning light inside your heart.

Who are the people watching?
Why aren't they helping? A nurse tapes an intravenous tube
to the boy, to feed him. The nurse's hands are human,
but the father's hands are the river the boy's
body floats in.

2

Two women pray. They are made of branches and twigs.
One holds a stick thick as a club.
The other weeps through clenched teeth as she begs Jesus to come.
The sky is a featureless milk-white above them.

One and a half million people
trying to live on the few seeds that fall from the sky,
air-dropped by the World Food Program.
You can see a man in a button down white shirt just looking on.

3

One mercenary pulls the baby
away from his screaming mother and tosses him
into the air—and another mercenary
shoots the boy like a clay pigeon.
A world falls out of the world before the baby
hits the ground.

III. The Ticking of Snow

To the Rich

1

Carried in her mother's beautiful arms
the dead daughter drifts past the season of wooden spoons in your kitchen.

She leaves a sadder, more holy, space than between any grazing horses.

She becomes a skeleton, a knot of bones, an untied knot of bones,
fragments of bones. Her tender flesh forms the corners of The Pentagon.

She cannot die of pleasure, be on time, see her own hair.
She cannot believe her clothing could be made of stars.

She cannot stand behind an easel, to paint you.

2

These babies are merciless telegrams you send yourself.
You set them adrift in the boats of their deaths.
They arrive at the shoreline of *afterwards* and step out on land alone.

They know their foreheads have failed.
They fly like moths against street lights, hitting the sealed flame of life.

The Ticking of Snow

1

      On the bureau, blue porcelain
        figurines of elephants face each other, like twin glyphs.
The air holds privacy, yet language,
          a soliloquy of light.
      An orchid floats away into its own echo.

This is a structure of grace.
      The pine branches outside the window seem a cloth frayed
          by today's moaning wind.

When rain abates, hollowness remains.

2

      A walnut wood cross
hangs on a nail by the kitchen window. The cross's crossbar needs dusting:
        the central air system's filter needs changing.

I try to imagine a small man nailed to the cross,
        but look instead at the dogwood tree outside my window. My uncle John
    died there,
shoveling snow. His body lay,

snow falling on his hair,
      and falling on his left wrist, bare between the sleeve and glove.
    My mother saw that, and told me. She said his wrist
was his last letter home.

*

    My question is not why, but *how* to pray
so all things hold together, without loss,
with love,
    how to venerate snowfall on the open eyes of my Uncle John,
and on so many dead children. I try imagining bells of snow

    so thin they tick against the bodies,
as if I could look away for a moment, and just listen
       to a machine counting. Then I try thinking the snow is an angels' song;
but like my mother, I look at the dead. And like her, I see them reaching back.

Icons

I-Skeleton of a Deer

1

Around noon, the bones
show through the snow, as the freeze
loosens its hold.

2

The cold
fades away around the antlers
first. Then the rib cage

(almost softly,
like rare white flowers, orchids of bone)
appears. This was a deer

left silent by dark, and ice-crusted snow,
and it waited. Now I hear
the bones burn with daylight.

3

I touch skull,
the clean eye sockets,
with my fingertip.

I close my eyes,
to make the air bear
us both.

4

Later, I sit looking at a silo
and lonely road.
How many deaths have struck that metal shape

and gone on?
For the first time, I see
the silo as a shadowy pool.

II-Christ

Your pale skin, your dark clothes,
your first two fingers raised in prayer,
your left eye slightly narrowed, the pupil enlarged,
the socket more rounded, your black
hair, your black beard, you seem destroyed,
an angel of compassion. I love you.

You cradle a thick book with your left arm.
The book's cover is gold, bearing a black cross
and small white circles, and the book is strapped shut
with three straps. There is a gold arc
behind your head. Your lips are pursed
in knowledge, and desire.

The left side of your face is in shadow,
darkest on your cheek. Does it hide a bruise, a scar?
You look straight at me, but I think you are not you,
and I am not I, as if we are both made of winter grass.
Our praying leans us like wind-bent stalks
toward the life beyond all seasons.

Photo of a Burial Bag

Some afternoons the light seems made of human skin, far off.
There seems a hand of light over the hills, fingertips of light
        touching the stones.
        Maybe Christ is *human skin*.

        There is a baby in a canvas bag
about to be buried. You can see the shadows of grown ups,
        but the body bag lies by itself on the dirt.

There are shoe prints around the horrid package.
Why is anyone going anywhere?
        Every detail of the bag shows up in the sunlight.

IV. Trying to Take Joy

*"Antonio Machado follows the moon
down a road of white dust,
to a cave of silent children
under the Pyrenees."*
   —James Wright

"You have to allow yourself to take joy."
   —Ruth Stone

Trying to Find Joy, Circa 1969

1-Wool Coat

She turns her back to the wind. This poem takes place
in a small land in which the raised collar
of her pea coat stands like a background hill.

She draws the match across the strike
pad, then cups the flame between her palms
against the wind. She leans toward her hands.
The fire leaps into the cigarette as she draws, then breaks free.

She shakes the flame out, drops the dark match.
Smoke from her lips catches in the wind, and is gone, lost.
She lifts her head, puts the match pack
back into her pocket, turns to me, takes another drag
and says, "Let's get some wine."

2-About Her Hands

This is about
her hands. They were thick
and beautiful, palms
I wanted on my skin
until I slept, while, maybe,
it was raining, and I listened to the rain turn,
like a huge page of parchment.

And maybe I looked at the dresser mirror
in our room on Sixth, lit by dim light
from a street light shining through rain,
and I saw her blouse on a chair
and I was glad she unbuttoned it and took it off
and put herself against me.

3-Poem for Garcia Lorca

2 pm. We're sitting in The Cypress Lounge
and she says goodbye. She walks out the door and by the window,
and I watch her. She walks across the street to a train station
and boards the Panama Limited. That day has folded
and refolded in my mind until the memory feels like a star
in my body. I had been in love and full of sadness and strange beauty,
and then after she left I gave it up to *think*,
like ringing a thousand pound bell.

There is a vase-like quality in loving the past. *I watch the rain hit the window.*
Between the rain and the window there is a third thing. It is Jesus walking on the sea.
I think something has been constructed toward me, from God.
Not a bridge, maybe a city. I sit here waiting for a hundred streets to arrive,
on schedule, *because it's God*. There's so much weight in the air, it's a blessing.
I have been against the earth getting tamed, by presence or absence,
and God's tropism toward me has been to send me a city. *Selah.*

Bourbon. I take the first sip and my heart flashes.
I like alcohol; it is Sevilla, waiting to ambush me, as Garcia Lorca says.
He also said dust in the wind makes "prows of silver,"
proras de plata. Believe this, Garcia Lorca: In the round mirror of the heart
all paths lead to a pale horse walking over a sheet of white light.

The Son She Left, 1977

*"Let the little children come to me, and do not hinder them,
for the kingdom of God belongs to such as these."*
—*Luke 18: 16*

Terrible, screaming rabbits,
flung burning from kerosened brush,
run back
into the black-tipped flames,
knowing only home defeats terror.

As this dazzles me,
something startled streaks out of mind
and leaves me helpless,
revealed and dead still,
like heartwood in a fallen tree.

And when you, son,
my flesh and question,
come asking,

I see in the pupils of your eyes
a beatable man, aflame with love,
loved.

But as I explain, holding you,
shelter and sheltering settles us,
to be in the final silence
the purer part, the hole in fire.

How I Feel

"He will repay the islands their due."
—Isaiah 59: 18

1

I like thin old men, and old wood floors,
in cafés with small tables near a window viewing the street, or sea.
If a street, it must be sunny, a few chairs set outside near the door.

I like two kinds of waiters.
One, an old man with grandchildren, who moves slowly and efficiently,
who owns the place.
The other, a young man, maybe a teenager
who talked all night with his girlfriend and who is full of intensity
about what's the right thing to do in his life.

I like sighs that escape the lips after the first sip of strong coffee.
I like white cups with fragile handles.

If by the sea, I like a striped awning and a flagpole, maybe a stone patio,
and a motorcycle parked in the area,
visible from the front door, and a rider who grew up there.
I like a stack of saucers and upside down cups behind the counter.

2

I pray for the deep
inside of a horse I saw
once, where a small scene
was carefully dying. The
river behind his eyes was
almost dry. The slow hiss
of leaves had gone from
his skin. And nothing else
remained, or ever was.

I wish that place a new
season with west wind, rain
and willow leaves.

3

And to you who pull the children down from the moon
and pave your driveways with their bones,

may the savaged moon be tied to your hearts
with braids of fire, and may you come to God
before God comes to you.

Other Titles From
ELIXIR PRESS

Circassian Girl
  by Michelle Mitchell-Foust

Imago Mundi
  by Michelle Mitchell-Foust

Distance From Birth
  by Tracy Philpott

Original White Animals
  by Tracy Philpot

Flow Blue
  by Sarah Kennedy

Monster Zero
  by Jay Snodgrass

Drag
  by Duriel E. Harris

Running the Voodoo Down
  by Jim McGarrah

Assignation at Vanishing Point
  by Jane Satterfield

The Jewish Fake Book
  by Sima Rabinowitz

Recital
  by Samn Stockwell

Murder Ballads
  by Jake Adam York

Puritan Spectacle
  by Robert Strong

Keeping the Tigers Behind Us
  by Glenn J. Freeman

Bonneville
  by Jenny Mueller

Fiction Titles

How Things Break
  by Kerala Goodkin

Limited Edition Chapbooks

Juju
  Judy Moffett

Grass
  Sean Aden Lovelace

X-Testaments
  Karen Zealand

Rapture
  Sarah Kennedy

Green Ink Wings
  Sherre Myers

Orange Reminds Me Of Listening
  Kristen Abraham

*In What I Have Done
& What I Have Failed To Do*
  Joseph P. Wood